BRIGHT IDEA BOOKS

SHAPESHIFTERS

by Meg Gaertner

CAPSTONE PRESS
a capstone imprint

Bright Idea Books are published by Capstone Press
1710 Roe Crest Drive, North Mankato, Minnesota 56003
www.mycapstone.com

Library of Congress Cataloging-in-Publication Data
Library of Congress Cataloging-in-Publication Data is available on the Library of Congress website.
ISBN: 978-1-5435-7125-7 (library hardcover)
978-1-5435-7502-6 (paperback)
978-1-5435-7137-0 (eBook PDF)

All internet sites appearing in back matter were available and accurate when this book was sent to press.

Editorial Credits
Editor: Claire Vanden Branden
Designer: Becky Daum
Production Specialist: Colleen McLaren

Photo Credits
Alamy: Album, 26–27, Erasmus Finx/AF Fotografie, 24; iStockphoto: Callipso, 20–21, lleerogers, 16–17, Lorado, 10–11, mjohnson, 13; Newscom: akg-images/Herbert Kraft, 7, Album/Metropolitan Museum of Art, NY, 9; Shutterstock Images: Bokasana, 19, 28, Brian A Smith, cover (bear), DavidTB, 15, Dean Drobot, cover (man), Nejron Photo, 30–31, Rudmer Zwerver, 5, Tom Tom, cover (forest), Wildlife World, 23

Design Elements: Shutterstock Images, Red Line Editorial

Printed in the United States of America.
PA70

TABLE OF CONTENTS

CHAPTER 1

SHAPESHIFTERS

A man's body changes. He becomes smaller. His teeth grow sharper. His arms become wings. He was human. Now he is a bat. He is a shapeshifter.

Many **cultures** around the world have **legends** of shapeshifters. These beings can change form. Some are animals that become humans. Other times humans turn into animals. Others are gods that change form.

In some stories other creatures can be shapeshifters, such as vampires. Many vampires can change into bats.

A LONG HISTORY

Trois Frères is a cave in France. Ancient paintings cover the walls. Many images are 14,000 years old. Some images show strange creatures. They are half human and half animal. Early humans may have believed in shapeshifters. Over time each culture told its own stories.

One drawing in the Trois Frères cave might show a person dressed as a goat.

CHAPTER 2

HUMAN Shapeshifting

Many stories tell of people turning into animals. Sometimes people change by choice. Other times they are **cursed**. Many **fairy tales** describe these curses. One story tells of a prince who turns into a frog. A prince turns into a beast in another story. These curses are often broken by love.

Beauty and the Beast is a popular story about a man shapeshifting into an ugly beast.

Many tales told of Viking warriors who went berserk during battle.

WEREWOLVES

Many stories talk about werewolves. These are people who turn into wolves. Some can change by choice. Others change during the full moon.

BERSERKERS

In other stories shapeshifters used their power to kill. A **Norse myth** describes the berserkers. These men were strong fighters. They wore wolf or bearskins. They went into a trance in battle. They went out of control, or "berserk." Some stories say they turned into wolves or bears. They killed many people. The first werewolf stories may have come from the berserkers.

SKINWALKERS

The Navajo people talk about skinwalkers. These are healers who have become evil. They can become coyotes, foxes, or wolves. Sometimes they become crows or owls. They can become any animal they want.

Skinwalkers try to hurt or scare people. There is one way to get rid of them. People can find a skinwalker's real name. Then they speak that name out loud. The skinwalker will die or get sick.

Stories say skinwalkers can become foxes.

CHAPTER 3

LOOKING Human

Many cultures describe shapeshifting creatures. These beings can **transform** into humans. They often look human to cause trouble. Other times they change for love.

In some stories people can transform into cats.

SELKIES

Irish and Scottish myths talk about selkies. They swim in the ocean as seals. Then they come onto land. They take off their sealskin. Suddenly the selkies look human. They must put on their skin to return to the sea.

There are stories of humans trapping selkies. A human man takes the skin of a selkie woman. She cannot return to the sea. She becomes the man's wife. Years later she finds her skin. She leaves the man for the ocean.

In many stories, selkies spend most of their time in water. The time they can spend on land willingly may be limited.

DOLPHIN SHAPESHIFTERS

Pink river dolphins swim in the Amazon River. One myth says they turn into men at night. They might kidnap people. They take people to an underwater city.

KITSUNE

Japanese **folklore** describes the kitsune. It is a Japanese fox demon. It tricks people by looking human. Sometimes it appears helpless. A person stops to help. The kitsune steals from that person. But a kitsune does not always play tricks. It can be thankful when people help it.

Other times the kitsune appears as a beautiful lady. It marries a human man. Many stories say the kitsune can create **illusions**. It makes people see things that are not there.

According to Japanese folklore, kitsune are very smart and creative.

STAYING SAFE

Kitsune cannot always hide their tails. Their tails may appear in the mirror. This shows what they really are.

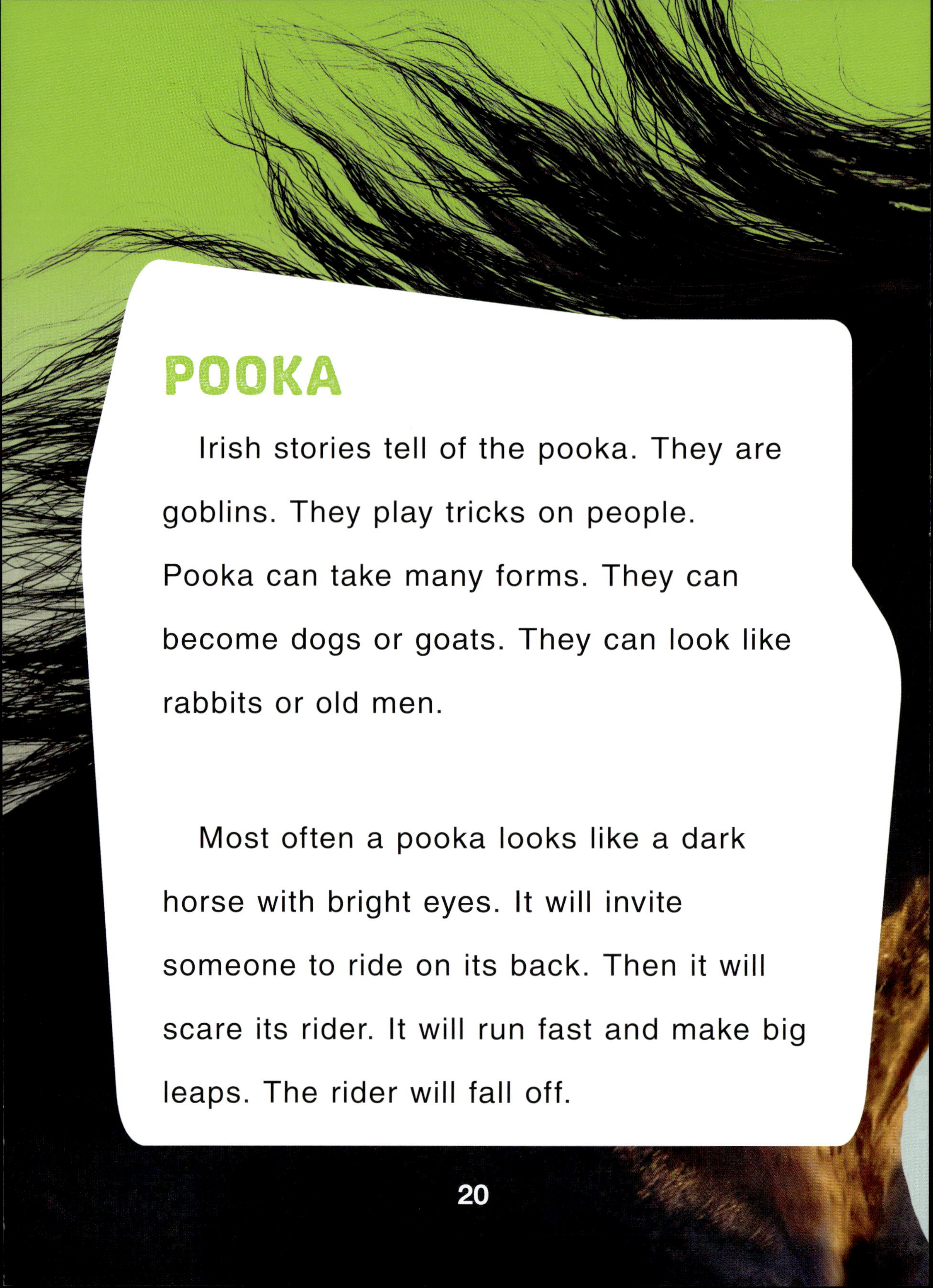

POOKA

Irish stories tell of the pooka. They are goblins. They play tricks on people. Pooka can take many forms. They can become dogs or goats. They can look like rabbits or old men.

Most often a pooka looks like a dark horse with bright eyes. It will invite someone to ride on its back. Then it will scare its rider. It will run fast and make big leaps. The rider will fall off.

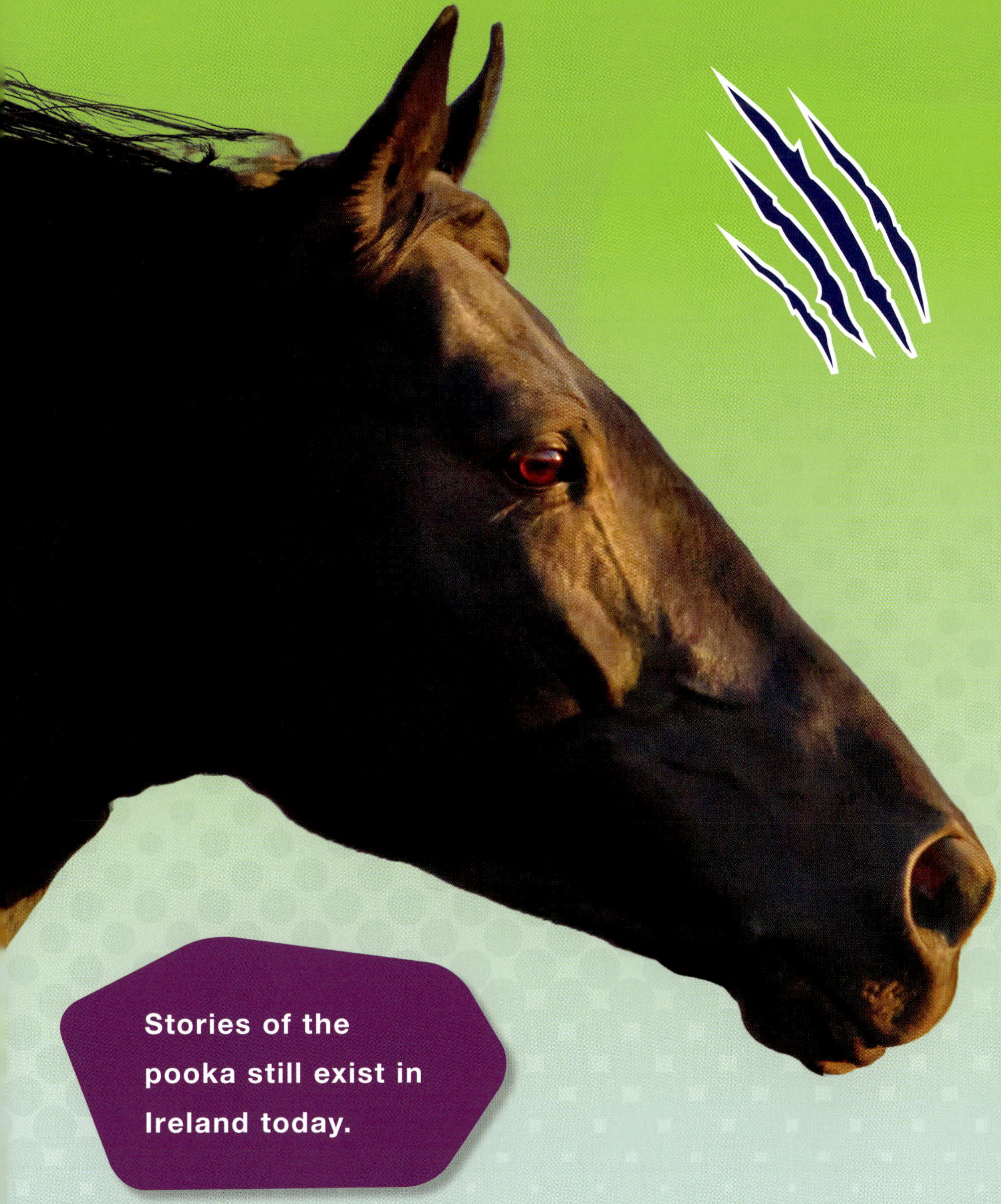

Stories of the pooka still exist in Ireland today.

CHAPTER 4

SHAPESHIFTING Gods

Some ancient peoples believed in shapeshifting gods. Zeus was the leader of the Greek gods. He often turned into animals. He used these forms to meet women.

In one story Zeus turned into a cuckoo bird to meet a woman.

Proteus could turn into many animals quickly.

Proteus was a sea god. He was a wise old man. Many people came to him. They wanted to know the future. They tried to catch him. But Proteus would escape. He changed into many animals to get away.

Loki would change form to cause trouble.

NORSE GODS

Loki was the Norse god of mischief. He could change his form. He used his shapeshifting to trick people. Odin was another Norse god. He could turn into an eagle.

GLOSSARY

culture
the set of beliefs and rules followed by a group of people

curse
an evil spell

fairy tale
a children's story about magical creatures

folklore
stories and beliefs passed down from generation to generation in a community

illusion
something that appears to be real but is not actually real

legend
a story that people say is true but that is not fully based on fact

myth
a story told by people in ancient times; myths often tried to explain natural events

Norse
relating to the people or language of medieval Scandinavia

transform
to make a big change in form or looks

TRIVIA

1. One legend from the Philippines talks of the Aswang. This creature is a mix between a vampire and a witch. It appears human during the day. It can turn into a deadly dog or beast at night.

2. The Slavs lived in Eastern Europe in ancient times. Their stories spoke of the leshy. This forest creature can appear in many forms. It can look like an old man. It can turn into a plant or animal. A leshy is a trickster. It makes people get lost in the forest.

3. The Algonquins are from Eastern Canada. One of their beliefs speaks of the wiitiko. In some stories it is a spirit that takes over humans. In other stories humans become the wiitiko if they eat other humans. A wiitiko is driven to eat human flesh.

ACTIVITY

WRITE A MYTH

Ancient cultures told stories about their history or beliefs. Many of these stories involved shapeshifters. Write a myth about a shapeshifter. Is your being a human or a creature? What does your being turn into and why? Then draw pictures of your creature in its different forms. Share your story and drawings with family and friends.

FURTHER RESOURCES

Want to know more about different myths? Learn more here:

DK Findout! Ancient Greek Gods and Goddesses https://www.dkfindout.com/us/history/ancient-greece/ancient-greek-gods-and-goddesses

Pearson, Marie. *Loch Ness Monster*. Monster Histories. North Mankato, Minn.: Capstone Press, 2020.

Curious about other monsters and shapeshifters? Check out these resources:

DK Findout! Viking Gods and Goddesses https://www.dkfindout.com/us/history/vikings/viking-gods

McCollum, Sean. *Werewolves: The Truth Behind History's Scariest Shape-Shifters*. Monster Handbooks. North Mankato, Minn.: Capstone Press, 2016.

Peterson, Megan Cooley. *Super Scary Monsters*. Super Scary Stuff. North Mankato, Minn.: Capstone Press, 2017.

INDEX